Compassion

Compassion

The Story of Clara Barton

by

Deborah Woodworth

Illustrated by

Leon Baxter

The Child's World®

Library of Congress Cataloging-in-Publication Data
Woodworth, Deborah.
Clara Barton: a story of compassion / Mary Logue.
p. cm.
Summary: Narrates the life of a small, shy nurse whose compassion
for others led her to fight for the establishment of the American Red
Cross

ISBN 1-56766-227-7

1. Barton, Clara, 1821-1912--Juvenile literature.
2. Red Cross--United States-- Biography--Juvenile literature.
3. Nurses--United States--Biography--Juvenile literature.
[1. Barton, Clara. 1821-1912. 2. American National Red Cross. 3. nurses. 4. Women--Biography.] I. Title.
HV569.B3W66 1996
361, 7'634'092
[B]--DC20
95-42271
CIP
AC

Contents

Clara's First Patient

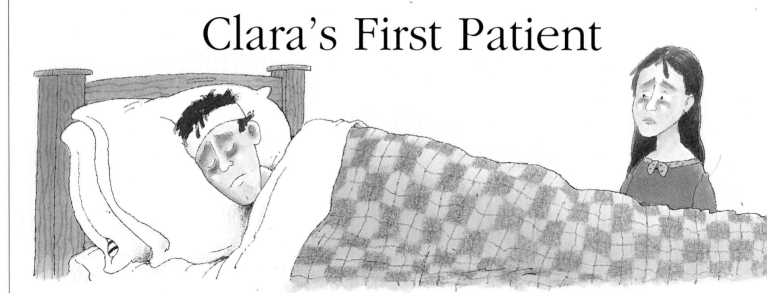

Eleven-year-old Clara Barton sat by the bedside of her favorite brother, David. He was gravely ill after falling from a barn roof. Clara had nursed David for nearly two years, but he was growing weaker and weaker. The doctors were losing hope. Yet Clara refused to give up on her brother. She stayed home from school to help him. And Clara liked school!

In 1832, doctors thought people could get sick because they had too much blood. They used leeches, which look like slimy worms, to suck out the extra blood. Clara had to stick them to her brother's skin. She did it because the doctors said it would help, but she did not like it. The leeches did not help David at all!

"I'm afraid there is nothing we can do," the doctors said. "We have tried leeches and our strongest medicines, but he keeps getting weaker. He is going to die."

"No!" Clara cried. "I'll nurse him until he is better, for as long as it takes. Somehow he'll get well."

Finally, another doctor told the family that bleeding would not help David get well. Clara was happy to throw out those leeches! The new doctor treated her brother with exercise and nutritious food. After a few weeks of the new doctor's treatment, David got better. Clara went back to school.

What Is *compassion?*

The dictionary defines *compassion* as "sorrow for the sufferings or trouble of another or others, accompanied by an urge to help." How is that different from pity? If you pity people, you feel sorry for them. But *compassion* means more. It also means wanting to help. Clara gave her time and her care to help her brother get well.

Growing Up

Clarissa Harlowe Barton was born on December 25, 1821, on a farm near Oxford, Massachusetts. Clara was short and thin. She had long, dark brown hair that flew behind her as she rode horses bareback. With two older sisters and two older brothers, Clara was always learning something new. From her brothers she learned to ride horses fearlessly and to hammer a nail in straight the first try. Her sisters were both teachers, and they taught her to read before she went to school at the age of four. Her mother taught her to cook and sew and to be practical.

Her father's stories, though, fascinated Clara. Captain Stephen Barton told her dozens of sad and exciting stories about his years as a soldier fighting the Indians and settling the West. From him, Clara learned how much soldiers and war victims suffered from lack of food and medical care.

"Once I was injured and starving in the wilds of Michigan," he told her. "I survived only by drinking the water that bubbled up in a horse's hoof print. All I could find to eat was a dog."

Clara listened and remembered. Everything she learned turned out to be useful in the years ahead, as she helped the sick and injured.

Clara was a shy child. Her family worried about her. She was timid around strangers and she would not speak up for herself. One winter day in church, her feet went numb from the cold. She stumbled and fell when she tried to walk.

"Why didn't you tell us how cold you were?" asked her father.

"I didn't want to bother anyone," Clara said.

But when someone needed her help, then she could be brave.

A School for Poor Children

In the 1830s, many American children went to school in one-room schoolhouses. Teachers had to pass a test, but they did not have to go to college. Clara loved to learn, so she decided to be a teacher in her hometown.

She faced her first class when she was only 17. Some of the boys were bigger than she was. She was so nervous, her knees shook! But soon she relaxed. The students liked her, and she liked teaching them.

In 1850, she decided to attend the Clinton Liberal Institute in New York to improve her knowledge. After finishing her studies, she began to teach in Bordentown, New Jersey. She taught in the only school in town, a private school. Parents paid a fee for their children to attend.

Clara was upset to find many of the town's poorer children roaming the streets, without a school to attend. New Jersey required free education for children, but many wealthy families did not like the idea of a free public school. They did not want their children to go to a "pauper school."

"Then I will open a public school," Clara decided. "I will create a school that all children can go to, no matter how poor they are—even if I have to teach for no pay!"

Clara Barton marched to the school board and fought for her plan. At first, they told her she was foolish.

"Those children would only end up in prison," they said. "Why should we waste free schooling on them?"

Clara was timid, but she was tough, too—and stubborn! In the end, she got her way. She was allowed to teach in an old, shabby school building. Clara and a few friends taught for free until the school board finally agreed to pay them for their work. The school became so popular that even the wealthy families sent their children. A new, bigger schoolhouse had to be built!

When the school grew to 600 students, the school board decided to put a man in charge. They thought the job was too big for a woman, even though Clara had been running the school all along.

Clara was angry and hurt. She resigned from the school and left teaching forever.

A less shy person might have stayed and fought the school board when they hired a man instead of her. Why did Clara give up and leave teaching? All her life, she had trouble fighting for herself alone. But she could stop being shy and speak out when others were in trouble. Her deep *compassion* gave her strength.

Angel of the Battlefield

It was 1854, and Clara needed a job. She moved to Washington, D.C., and became a copyist for the U.S. Patent Office. In those days, there were no copy machines. Documents had to be copied by hand. It was dull work, but Clara earned money that she later used for her next big project.

While she lived in Washington, trouble was brewing between the northern and southern states. In 1861, the Civil War began. Clara watched soldiers from her hometown of Oxford go off to fight. She was worried. They had no extra rations. They had no towels or soap or handkerchiefs. How could they help themselves if they were wounded? So she used her own money to buy them soap. She tore up her own sheets to make them towels and handkerchiefs. Then she convinced other people to contribute, too.

When the Civil War began, an injured soldier might lie on the battlefield for days. He would lie there without food or water, waiting for medical treatment. Doctors had to work in filthy conditions, without enough medicine or bandages. Many soldiers died from hunger and exposure to the cold and the rain.

Clara decided to go to the battle front to help. Shy as she was, Clara argued and pleaded with government officials, all the way up to the Surgeon General. As usual, she got her way in the end.

Clara planned carefully. She gathered supplies from hundreds of people. She stuffed a wagon with crates and boxes and barrels. They were full of bandages, medicines, crackers, canned meats, jams, and even wine to help deaden pain.

She soon arrived at her first battlefield—Cedar Mountain in Virginia. The doctors had already used up all their medical supplies. When Clara dug into her boxes and dragged out linen bandages, the army surgeon nicknamed her "The Angel of the Battlefield."

Some problems seem so bad that we want to solve them right away. Clara wanted to help the doctors and soldiers quickly. What if she had not thought much about what to bring? What if she had just jumped on a horse and raced to the battlefield? In the end, she was more help to the soldiers because she took some time to plan.

In September of 1862, Clara took her supply wagon to the Battle of Antietam, where 26,000 soldiers died. Clara made her way through the battlefield, delivering food and first aid to thousands of wounded. Bullets whizzed past her. One bullet went through her sleeve as she reached out to an injured soldier.

A soldier in pain pleaded with Clara to remove a musket ball from his cheek. She hesitated.

"But I'm not a doctor," she protested. "I'll hurt you, and I have nothing to numb the pain."

The soldier begged her to help him.

Nervously, Clara opened her clean pocketknife. Another wounded man held the patient's head, and Clara cut out the bullet.

"I have had a barrel of apple sauce made today and given out every spoonful of it with my own hands. I have cooked ten dozen eggs, made cracker toast, cornstarch blanc mange [a pudding], . . . washed hands and faces, put ice on hot heads, mustard on cold feet, written six soldiers' letters home, stood beside three death beds. . . ." —*Clara Barton*

Lost Soldiers

Before Clara left for the battlefields, a soldier named Mr. Farley had visited her. He was about to leave for the battle front. His girlfriend was waiting for him back in Indiana. If Clara read that he had been killed, he asked, would she send a letter to his girl?

On the battlefield, many injured and dying soldiers asked the same favor of Clara. She understood the pain of families who longed to know whether their loved ones were alive or dead. Clara's own brother, Stephen, was mistakenly arrested by Union soldiers. He was kept as a prisoner of war. For years, Clara had no word of him. Finally, a letter from Stephen reached her. With the help of a government official, Clara got him released. He was seriously ill. She nursed him, but he never recovered.

The Civil War ended in 1865. Clara went back to Washington with a new mission. She wanted to form an organization to let families know the fates of their missing loved ones. As she often did, Clara used her own money to get started.

Clara worked for four years to locate 22,000 missing soldiers. Many of these men were buried at Andersonville, Georgia, in a Confederate prison camp. Only numbers marked their graves. One prisoner had secretly kept a list of the dead soldiers' names. He sewed it into the lining of his coat to sneak it out of the camp. Clara was now able to tell their families where the soldiers were buried.

"Ease pain, soothe sorrow, lessen suffering." —*Clara Barton*

An Adventure in Europe

After the Civil War ended, Clara was worn out and got very sick. Her doctors insisted that she travel to Europe to recover her health. In 1869, she packed and left for a long rest. But Clara Barton had a way of finding people who were suffering.

Only a month after she arrived in Switzerland, several men came to visit her. They told her about an organization called the Red Cross. Red Cross workers gave food, clothing, and medical help to victims of war, no matter which side the victims were on. Most of Europe had signed the Geneva Treaty to join the Red Cross. Because the Red Cross workers did not take sides, they were allowed to go anywhere without being shot or arrested.

Clara was delighted! She wanted to bring this wonderful organization to the United States. There was just one problem. The American government had already refused to sign the Geneva treaty and join the Red Cross.

Soon Clara had a chance to work with the Red Cross. Within a few months, war broke out between France and Prussia. Clara was asked to help. She quickly forgot how tired she was! Instead of resting, she traveled through Germany and France, helping soldiers and citizens from both countries.

The work was dangerous. In one small town, Clara was thought to be a spy! German soldiers demanded to see her credentials. One drunken soldier threatened her with his sword, but Clara would not show fear. Finally, he left her alone.

Clara made her way to Strasbourg, a French city the Germans had captured. The city was in ruins. Men, women, and children were badly wounded. Thousands had lost their homes and were wandering the streets, hurt and starving.

The Grand Duke of Baden, Germany, had conquered Strasbourg. His wife, the Grand Duchess, wanted to help the people her husband had defeated. She asked Clara to give away gifts of money. Clara thought these gifts were a mistake. She wanted the people of Strasbourg to be able to work again. She wanted them to feel that they had rebuilt their own city.

Clara convinced the Grand Duchess to let her pay the people of Strasbourg to repair their city. She gathered the women together and put them to work. They cut fabric and sewed clothes for everyone in Strasbourg. Clara paid the women for their work, so they were able to begin saving money again.

Charity is one helpful way to show *compassion*. But what happens when the donations of money, food, and clothing are gone? Clara showed that people could be helped even more when they could help themselves. By paying the women of Strasbourg to make clothes, Clara gave them more than just clothes and money. She helped them start working again for their own future.

The American Red Cross

Clara returned home in 1873, determined to form an American branch of the Red Cross. Little did she know how hard this would be! It took her nine years to convince the government to sign the Geneva treaty. During those years, Clara worked long and hard. She pleaded her cause with senators and statesmen and even three presidents.

At first, no one would listen. American officials did not want to join with the European nations. They believed the United States would never again be at war. So why should they want an organization meant to help war victims?

Clara believed that the Red Cross could do much more than just help during wartime. Every year, people were injured or driven from their homes by floods, forest fires, tornadoes, and hurricanes. They had nowhere to go. No one provided food, shelter, or first aid for victims of these natural disasters.

When Clara pleaded the cause of the Red Cross, she emphasized how helpful it could be during peacetime as well as war. This idea was all her own. In Europe, the Red Cross was active only during wars.

Clara had taken on the government before. She knew how to be stubborn, if that's what it took! Finally, her efforts paid off. Robert Lincoln, son of the late President Abraham Lincoln, promised to help Clara. In 1881, President Garfield pledged his support to the Red Cross.

Clara felt so hopeful that she started forming local Red Cross chapters. She wanted them to be ready as soon as the United States signed the Geneva treaty.

In 1881, Congress finally approved the treaty. The bill was sent to the president to sign.

But on July 2, President James A. Garfield was shot by an assassin. The Geneva treaty lay unsigned on his desk.

After President Garfield's death, Clara had a chance to show everyone how useful the Red Cross could be. A huge forest fire in northern Michigan injured many people and left about 5,000 homeless.

Several local chapters of the Red Cross had just been formed. They were ready to help the fire victims. Clara turned her own home into her headquarters and directed the Red Cross volunteers. She pleaded for help from citizens. Money and supplies came in from all over the country.

Clara had finally proved her case. Congress was convinced that the Red Cross was worthwhile. In March of 1882, Congress approved the Geneva treaty. President Chester Arthur signed the bill and it became a law.

At the age of 60, when most people are thinking about retiring, Clara Barton became President of the American Red Cross.

What makes a small, shy person brave enough to dodge musket bullets on a battlefield? How did Clara Barton find the courage to march into presidents' offices to fight for the Red Cross? Some people accomplish a lot out of anger or love, or maybe because they are greedy. Clara did jobs that were hard for her because she wanted so badly to help people who were suffering. Her *compassion* for others was stronger than her fears.

Study Guide

Reading about famous or successful people can help us live our own lives. Sometimes we learn from their achievements, and sometimes we learn from their setbacks. Clara Barton experienced both.

1. Which of these qualities do you think are most important?

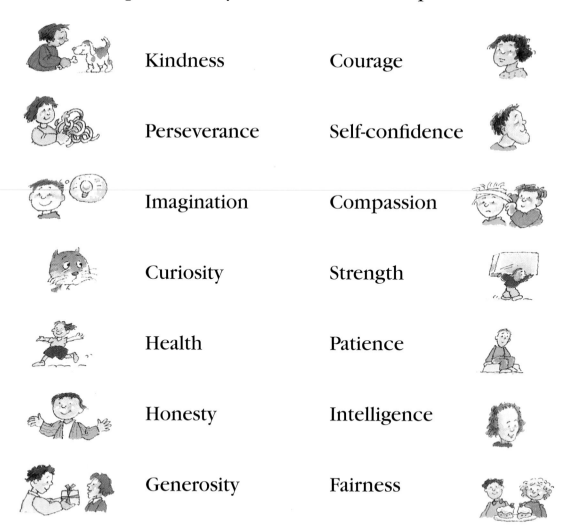

Kindness	Courage
Perseverance	Self-confidence
Imagination	Compassion
Curiosity	Strength
Health	Patience
Honesty	Intelligence
Generosity	Fairness

Which qualities do you think were most important to Clara Barton?

2. During her life, Clara Barton helped many people, like soldiers and flood victims. If Clara were alive today, whom do you think she would try to help?

3. Sometimes people didn't give Clara much help or support. How do you think she moved ahead to the next challenge?

4. Even as a girl, Clara showed a lot of compassion. She wanted to help her brother get well more than she wanted to learn or even to play outside. How do you think Clara's life would have been different if she had not been so compassionate?

5. Other compassionate people have tried to help the sick and the poor. Can you name any of them?

Study Guide Answers

1. Each of these qualities is just as important as the others. Clara Barton needed many of them to do everything that she did. Helping wounded soldiers during battles took great courage and strength. Compassion alone wasn't enough to help her start the American Red Cross. It took intelligence and imagination to show that the Red Cross could help in natural disasters and not just during wars. Without perseverance and patience, she wouldn't have found the graves of thousands of missing soldiers.

2. Today the American Red Cross is a huge organization. Red Cross workers help people during emergencies, such as wars or natural disasters. For example, after a hurricane, the Red Cross provides food, clothes, first aid, and a place to stay for people who have lost their homes.

   If Clara Barton were alive today, maybe she would try to open clinics for people who are sick and homeless. She might want to go to a country where there are many sick people and not enough doctors. Or maybe she would go to a country at war to nurse the wounded. What do *you* think?

3. Everyone wants to be appreciated for doing good. Clara formed Bordentown, New Jersey's first public school. Yet when it became popular, the school board appointed a man as superintendent, instead of Clara. Naturally Clara was angry! She resigned from the school. Then she began to look around to see where she would be needed next. Soon she started an

even bigger project, helping wounded soldiers. Creating the Bordentown school taught her that she could accomplish a lot when she set her mind to it. Clara didn't dwell too long on her disappointments. Her compassion pushed her forward.

4. Clara was so timid that she would not tell her family she was freezing in church. Yet she could be tough and determined when she was trying to help others. If she had not been so compassionate, she probably would have been shy all the time. She would not have been able to persuade the president when she wanted to start an American Red Cross. Maybe someone else would have started the American Red Cross, but not Clara. Her strong compassion helped her conquer her own shyness and make life better for so many people.

5. During the 1800s, it was very dangerous to be sick or wounded! Many hospitals were crowded and dirty. Most of the medicines we have today had not been developed yet. Dorothea Dix spent her life improving treatment of the insane, who were chained and treated like criminals. Florence Nightingale, an English woman, fought to make hospitals clean and free of germs.

In the 1900s, Albert Schweitzer went to Africa and used his own money to build a hospital for poor people. Mother Teresa has built clinics to help sick people in the slums of India. Maybe someone you know is trying to help people, too!

Clara Barton Time Line

December 25, 1821 Clarissa Harlowe Barton is born near Oxford, Massachusetts.

1832 Clara nurses her sick brother, David.

1838 Clara begins teaching.

1850 Clara attends the Clinton Liberal Institute in New York.

1852 Clara opens her free school in Bordentown, New Jersey.

1861 Clara begins working as a nurse during the Civil War.

1869 Clara travels to Europe. She meets with members of the European Red Cross.

1873 Clara Barton returns to the United States.

1882 The United States signs the Geneva Treaty. Now the United States could join the International Committee of the Red Cross.

April 12, 1912 Clara Barton dies of pneumonia.